Leeds Metropolitan University

17 0149722 9

BUSINESS
PLANS

BUSINESS PLANS

25 Ways to Get Yours Taken Seriously

BRIAN FINCH

KOGAN
PAGE

LEEDS METROPOLITAN
UNIVERSITY LIBRARY

1701497229
B9aDL
435901   2.8.96
24 9.90
658 4012 FIN

First published in 1992

Reprinted 1993, 1994 20

Apart from any fair dealing for the purposes of research or private
study, or criticism or review, as permitted under the Copyright,
Designs and Patents Act, 1988, this publication may only be
reproduced, stored or transmitted, in any form or by any means, with
the prior permission in writing of the publishers, or in the case of
reprographic reproduction in accordance with the terms of licences
issued by the Copyright Licensing Agency. Enquiries concerning
reproduction outside those terms should be sent to the publishers at
the undermentioned address:

Kogan Page Limited
120 Pentonville Road
London N1 9JN

© Blackstone Franks and Brian Finch 1992

British Library Cataloguing in Publication Data

A CIP record for this book is available from the British Library.

ISBN 0-7494-0870-7

Typeset by Books Unlimited (Nottm) – Sutton in Ashfield, NG17 1AL

Printed in England by Clays Ltd, St Ives plc

Contents

Introduction

You probably have a few minutes to make a good impression with your plan. That means that by the time the reader has finished the summary and maybe the introduction, you have won or lost.

What? You have no summary? You are not helping your case. You are already behind on points and trying to recover your position.

It is difficult to write a good business plan. It is a very specialised type of writing and you may only produce one or two in your career. Most business plans are not very good. This means that finance is harder to raise than it need be, business sales are delayed, business partners are harder to find, and the deal obtained is worse than could have been achieved.

You agree that improvement is possible or we wouldn't be talking to each other. Yes, we are talking to each other. Think of the business plan as a conversation, except that you have to explain clearly and answer the questions before they arise. If you do that well you will continue the conversation face to face.

This book is designed to assist business managers in writing better plans. It is written as for an entrepreneur raising finance but all the same considerations apply to the manager of a subsidiary of a large organisation. In that case the head office is the financier. There will be other considerations such as internal politics and strategic views of what businesses the group as a whole wishes to develop. But this is similar to the outlook of many venture capital funds which are also taking a view of how much they have invested in particular industries and how much exposure they want to have.

8 Business Plans

This book should also be of assistance to business people who want to draw up a business plan to guide the management of their business. It is a good approach to write your plan as if you were seeking finance. On the basis of what you have written would you, as an outsider, invest? Of course, there is no outside financier looking at your plan. You are both financier and manager.

For the entrepreneur, professional assistance will probably still be required, to give a detached perspective and to help with the numbers, but the managers or promoters of the business should try to produce the first draft. The document will form the basis for subsequent presentations: if the manager who has to talk about the plans is not totally familiar with them, then the case will not convince anyone.

This is not a recipe book. Every business is different but there is a basic minimum which is covered in the checklist in Appendix 1.

1. Start with a summary

Your audience is busy and will give you just a few minutes to be convincing. After that it is either straight in the bin or a quick skim so that they can say they have read it *or* you have got their attention.

> 'It's a long shot, but send me a plan ... I can read a plan in five minutes.'
>
> *Venture capitalist*

Your first objective is to grab the reader's attention; not with some gimmick but because the proposal is interesting.

The summary is your tool for grabbing attention. Before the reader knows it, he or she has been told the outline of your case and is interested. They want to know more detail: they read on, already willing to be convinced.

The summary should almost never be more than a page long. It does not include all the evidence of your case, only an outline of the most important points that encapsulate the story you have to tell. It says what the situation is and what is proposed. Write it after you have written the rest of the document. Since it is meant to summarise your story, you must finish that story before you can decide what to include. You need to decide the balance of points also.

Example

Summary

Qualco is a family-owned laundry and dry cleaning business, established in West London 25 years ago by the father of the current proprietor. Turnover has grown steadily in the past five years to £1.1 million and pre-tax profits to £160,000. A central laundry has been added this year to cope with demand. It has also reduced staff costs by 15 per cent.

There is market demand to add another two shops in the area which can be serviced by the central laundry and controlled by the existing management. They believe they would win business from local competitors who cannot compete on price or quality. The cost of establishing another two units is £300K, including pre-opening costs and up to six months of possible trading losses. Owing to other recent investments the business cannot finance this from cash flow. The owner proposes to invest another £50K and seeks £250K by means of a £100K secured loan and £150K of risk finance. The project shows a forecast return of 25 per cent per annum.

2. Why are you writing this plan?

There are four main reasons for writing a business plan:

- To raise finance from banks and investors
- To help to sell a business
- To find or retain a business partner or key employee
- As an aid to manage the business.

> 'The former chairman of three public companies sought to raise money to acquire a business in the industry he knew so well. Presumably relying on his track record, he refused to produce a business plan. Needless to say he could not obtain finance and lost the deal.'
>
> *Solicitor close to the chairman*

What is your objective? Focus on it and write with it in mind. For instance, don't produce a fund-raising document, setting out how you need money to achieve a blockbuster idea, if you are actually trying to sell the business. The purchaser may wonder why you are not sticking around if super opportunities are just opening up. Worse, if you have oversold yourself you may find the purchaser insisting that you stay.

Your objective is to get a decision of some kind from someone, as a result of their reading your document. That decision may be an agreement to meet you. If you meet you have an opportunity to sell them your idea in person and to demonstrate that you really know what you are talking about. Remember that you have already made your first impression through the document.

Focus also on what decision you want when writing your plan. If you seek a meeting then the document may be the wrong place to put masses of detail. Perhaps you should include a summary of your forecasts and keep the two inches of computer print-out until you are asked for it.

> 'There was one proposal I read recently that didn't tell me what they wanted and what their precise plans were. It was just vague. It didn't inspire confidence.'
>
> *Venture capitalist*

3. Who are you writing it for?

Think about your audience.

> 'I read this proposal from some academics working at a research institute. The biggest problem I had was that I couldn't understand the jargon so I still don't know what their work was all about. Even if it was a good idea they obviously can't communicate with the "real world" so they won't succeed.'
>
> *Corporate finance consultant*

This example is an extreme case but we all tend to forget our audience:

- Who are they?
- What do they want in a business plan?
- What language will they understand?

If you are talking to financiers you may need to include more financial information. If you are addressing the marketing director of a company which is a potential business partner, you may need to devote more time to explaining market synergies.

A bank manager will be most concerned about the security for a loan, while a venture capitalist may be more concerned to know how sensitive your projections are to things going a bit wrong or very well (how easily can venture capital money be lost and how large are the returns for taking a risk?). A business partner will want to see the areas for mutual benefit and co-operation.

Give the information that your audience needs. If you aren't sure who may read your plan try to cover the likely targets.

easy to use jargon that the reader will not understand. As in the example above, it may not only confuse but be a 'turn off' to the whole project. You may not know for certain who will receive your document. Proposals are often passed on by the original recipient. It may go from a general manager of a subsidiary to an acquisitions manager at head office. Try to use simple English and explain clearly concepts that an outsider to your trade may not understand. You can check your document by asking someone else to read it, someone who knows you but not your business. Can they understand your proposal? .

4. Make it easy

You have sent your plan to a prospective financier or to a planning director. This plan is the most important thing in your life at present. *Remember that it is not the most important thing in their lives!* They have each received four plans today; they have a lunch meeting and two further meetings booked for the afternoon. This morning there is a list of 12 telephone calls to make and four urgent memos to write, plus a regular departmental meeting. How much time do you think your plan has to make an impression?

- You are right ... *not long.*
- You have done the right thing and written a one-page summary of the key points in the plan and your proposals. This has captured the reader's attention, who turns the page. Continue to make it easy.
- If the plan is more than three or four pages long put in an index.
- Number the pages; maybe number the points as well.
- Don't waffle. If someone has to plough through pages and pages to get to the meat you will create a bad impression of yourself *and* turn them off.
- Set out the document so that it is easy to read; put in headings, put detail in appendices, use a clear type face (not a tiny print that the reader has to strain to read), space out paragraphs.
- Date the document to avoid confusion with earlier or later drafts.

Some people like to number each paragraph for easy reference. Some like to have a hierarchy of headings, for example:

MAIN HEADING

Sub-Heading

Sub-Sub-Heading

- If you can show diagrams or photographs of important products, premises, processes, etc, they will bring the subject alive for the reader.
- Whatever you do, don't spend ages producing a computer forecast which second guesses the financier's financial structure. You have probably got it wrong and the financier will have to rework it. Stop at the trading result.

I am greatly indebted to Professor Ehrenberg of the London Business School, who first introduced me to the obvious and simple idea that people do not take in lots of long numbers when they read a document. Why then do we put masses of confusing numbers in documents where we are trying to communicate ideas?

Test even someone who is used to dealing with pages of numbers, ask almost any accountant to quote numbers from a page they have just read. They will not tell you that 'Turnover was £3.176 million in 1986 while profits before tax were £0.1975 million'. If they remember at all they will have simplified the information to something like, 'Turnover in 1986 was £3.2 million and pre-tax profits were only £0.2 million'. Some meaning about relative size has been extracted, the word 'only' is in the accountant's reply.

This is the second important fact to remember: people take in information better when it has *meaning* for them. Make life easy, tell them the meaning, and they will take in what you are trying to tell them.

An experiment was conducted using professional chess players and novices. Chess pieces were carefully laid out on a board to simulate the middle of a game and the two groups were asked to memorise the positions of the pieces. The professionals did far better than the novices.

The experiment was repeated with the chess pieces set out at random. This time the professionals did not do appreciably better than the novices.

We take in and remember patterns and meaning far better than random jumbles of information. If you want a reader to take in the good points about your business and to remember and understand, then don't present confusion and jumbles of information.

Research shows that people tend to be able to take in the first two figures of numbers they scan on a page. So if we see;

   3,123,456   4,345,997   5,616,227

we are likely to take these in as:

   3.1 million   4.3 million   5.6 million

Why then do so many people produce tables of numbers in reports that are hard to take in and even harder to remember?

They do it because they have not thought through why they are putting the numbers on paper. They have forgotten that they are trying to communicate with someone. They may think that they are showing no respect for accuracy if they are not precise. The computer may throw out information that way, if so:

1. You may be able to get the computer to print out in a different way.
2. You can put the computer print-out in an appendix and print out summarised numbers in the report.
3. Who is writing this business plan, you or the computer?

For example:

Not ...

£	1990	1991	1992
Turnover	3249612	4755816	4873245
Gross profit	837146	947888	857930
Overheads	666987	734579	789002
Net profit	170159	213309	68928

with no explanation. And plans really do appear looking even worse than this.

but ...

£000	1990	1991	1992
Turnover	3,300	4,800	4,900
Gross profit	840	950	860
	(26%)	(20%)	(18%)
Overheads	670	730	790
	(21%)	(15%)	(16%)
Net profit	170	220	70

a   Turnover increased by 46 per cent in 1991 as a result of our price cutting but by only 2 per cent in 1992 when our competitors responded.

b   Gross profit declined from 26 to 18 per cent over the period owing to the lower prices.

c   Meanwhile we cut overheads in relative terms from 21 to 16 per cent of turnover.

While our strategy worked very well in the first year (profits up 24 per cent), the lack of growth in year two, continuing fall in margin and slight increase in overheads, led to a collapse in profits. We expect that this will be just as dramatically recovered, following the recent bankruptcy of our main competitor.

Continuing the theme of making life easy for the reader, be ready to communicate through graphs and diagrams rather than tables of numbers; they can often tell a story more effectively.

Example

Typical customer spend in £ per game

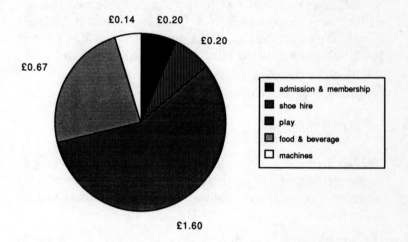

or

Number of bowling lanes in the UK

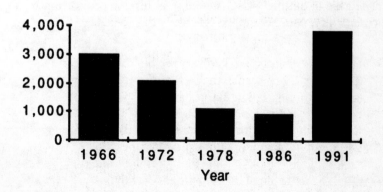

However, don't get carried away by gimmicks and flood your business plan with unnecessary pictures. Always ask, 'What is the most effective way of communicating this idea powerfully to my reader?'

Finally, having communicated the business concept and background, don't spoil it by formulating some complicated financial scheme using devices such as A Ordinary Shares, B Ordinary Shares, Preference Shares, Debentures, etc, and don't worry about how much is due to which, under what circumstances, why and when!

Observe two rules:

- Keep it simple.
- Leave room for negotiation.

Nobody invests in schemes they don't understand; most entrepreneurs overvalue their businesses; and, when confronted with what they interpret as take-it-or-leave-it, most investors will leave it.

Outline what you hope to achieve by all means but don't offer the solutions. Leave that to the professionals. It is bad enough once the lawyers get hold of your broad agreement and turn it into legal jargon and tell you why the scheme needs to be complicated. If you start with something complicated it will either get nowhere or get worse.

The ease of getting a deal signed is in inverse proportion to its complexity. More complex: less likely to succeed.

5. You are telling a story

You have captured your reader's attention; now you must keep it. You must also stimulate his enthusiasm for your project so that he will back you. The story of you, your business and what you propose to do with it is a fascinating story: tell it that way.

A story has a beginning, a middle and an end. The beginning is the background to your business and how you got here; the middle is what your business is all about, and the end is what you propose. A story grabs the attention of the reader and stimulates interest and imagination. It flows – so should a business plan.

If a plan is disjointed and hard to follow, like a story of the same kind it will lose the reader. To continue the comparison, you are not trying to write James Joyce's *Ulysses*, which few people start to read and fewer finish; you are trying to write a popular novel (but not quite so long). *There is no ideal length*. It all depends on the business. A small business can still be complicated and need a lot of explaining, while a large business can be comparatively simple. Just remember to be brief. Follow the rule of getting someone who knows nothing about your business or the market to read your plan. See if you have explained it clearly to them. Ask if it is too long.

As with a book, it is important to remember the plot, the descriptive bits (background or scene setting) and the characters. Your plans and background are essential but so are the people who will carry it all out. Some people get the balance wrong and waffle on endlessly about the market or about themselves, or about the history of the business. Remember balance and don't bore your reader.

6. 'We are the team to back!' – you are selling yourselves

Research shows that the most important factor for investors in evaluating a proposal is the management team they back.

> 'A good management team can "make it" in a poor market or a declining industry but a weak team won't survive even in a boom market.'
>
> *Venture capitalist*

If you aren't an impressive and balanced team think how you can address the issue; perhaps you should bring someone in to provide an area of skills you don't have.

The skills that you have should be presented well. Have a section in your plan about management. Tell the reader about the management team's individual responsibilities if these are not obvious.

Example

> **Peter Williams, Managing Director (age 52)**
> ... Has direct responsibility for sales to ANB ...
>
> **Alan Warter, Sales & MArketing Director (age 37)**
> ... Works closely with Peter Williams on marketing strategy and assists him with the ANB relationship ...

Give a very brief background of each of the top management team. For each person, give: their age, relevant academic or professional qualifications, experience in the industry and job they are doing or will do, highlights of past employment experience, share stake in the company if they have one.

Put down each person's *achievements* and emphasise career progression. Bring out their experience, qualifications and strengths that are relevant to their current or proposed role.

Example

John Smith BSc, FCCA, Finance Director (aged 41)
Joined the company as finance director in 1987, having been group financial controller with Jones Amalgamated plc from 1985 until its takeover by Mega Corporation in 1987. He was responsible for all financial reporting at Jones, was closely involved in their £120 million rights issue in 1986 and was part of the bid defence team. Previous experience includes two years as finance director of a £70 million turnover mechanical contracting subsidiary of Stronson plc, during which he oversaw installation of a new computer and accounting system.

Put a more detailed CV for each in an appendix. These should only be a page long but should give educational details and each employer; responsibilities and achievements gained in each job.

Some entrepreneurs are too proud to sell themselves; they give general background information, few hard facts. Maybe they are hiding something. It certainly puts the financier on guard, maybe without need. They may succeed despite this attitude, but why create problems? The better the story you volunteer, the better the impression you create and the less questioning you will be subjected to.

Show your organisational structure:

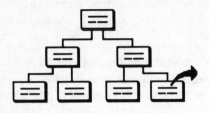

You are a team and an organisation and you must demonstrate the ability of both. Show how the organisation works and explain what is relevant. Give numbers of staff employed in particular areas to prove the level of responsibility of managers and that they are not overstretched.

> 'I was drafting a bid defence document once and found that one manager had 13 people reporting directly to him. That is too many for one person to manage effectively so we didn't show organisation charts after all.'
>
> *Merchant banker*

People are uneasy about backing one-man or one-woman companies but none the less the fact is that many businesses are driven by one powerful personality, especially in the early days. Will one or two key people become overloaded? What happens if one key individual is ill for a week? Does the whole enterprise grind to a halt?

Demonstrate an effective team which can at least cope with the day-to-day issues on its own.

> 'I had a great start-up proposal for a publishing company, headed by someone who had "done it before". Unfortunately, it wasn't for us; who would put all that money behind one person's judgement?'
>
> *Venture capitalist*

You can anticipate this problem by trying to set up with a partner or by having an identified team ready to join at the appropriate time.

Venture capitalists always seek references from previous business colleagues on management teams they back. Have yours ready and be sure they will say nice things.

> 'Jo gave two references from previous jobs. Both said he lacked attention to detail and one of them was not really very friendly at all. He should either have given other references or found a way to defuse the comments. His plan could have emphasised that Pete would deal with detailed day-to-day issues or he could have told us that he was not a detail man. At least the latter would have given him a chance to answer our concerns. We obviously didn't tell him why we turned down his project, we just said no, and he had no chance to challenge the evidence against him.'
>
> *Corporate finance consultant*

7. Facts → Numbers → Evidence

Someone who reads a business plan seeks confirmation, seeks evidence to persuade them that what they are reading is true. This should be provided by putting verifiable facts in the text wherever possible. These facts should be supported by numbers to set in context how relevant each fact is and to support the projections later in the report. *Provide evidence for what you say.*

> 'Start-ups are always hard to back. One reason is the limited evidence that is available to back the claims. One team told me about the number of potential outlets in the UK. One of them owns a chain of three. He had not given any evidence in the document to support his estimate of the number of outlets. Nor had he given data from his own business to support the sales assumptions. Nor had he conducted a survey of other similar businesses to support the sales assumptions. I had to rely on his word, which he repeated frequently … but which I felt was insufficient support.'
>
> *Venture capitalist*

It is a famous dictum of propaganda that a lie, if repeated frequently enough, becomes accepted as the truth eventually. It does not work in business plans or in face-to-face discussion. Constant repetition focuses the reader's attention on the issue and, if he does not believe an assertion, simply reinforces a climate of doubt and disbelief. *Give the facts to support your claims: don't simply repeat the claims.*

Whatever you do, don't waffle! It is common to read reports that go on at great length about the market, the opportunity, the history of the project, etc. This may be badly or beautifully written but it is all the same; it is not being written for the right audience. It is being written for the writer who is passionate about the business and very interested in him or herself. The attention of the business partner or divisional chief executive or financier was lost at the beginning, when they got bored and decided they didn't believe the hype.

Example

> Not ...
>
> This gigantic market is growing rapidly and will soon be absolutely vast and once we have conquered it in a couple of years' time we will start on the even more ginormous European market where there is even more potential and no competition and in any case nobody can copy our unique product.
>
> but ...
>
> The UK market is estimated to be worth approximately £220 million per annum and to be growing at about 17 per cent (*Financial Times* Survey 29 February 1991). If development follows the course of the USA, the potential market size is about £450 million, which gives considerable room for continued growth. Trade sources (see Appendix II) suggest that the current suppliers are finding difficulty meeting demand and backlogs have grown to 18 weeks or more. This supports our sales forecasts.
>
> We believe there are further opportunities for expansion in the European Community, where the market is at a similar stage of development to the UK four years ago. Our plans show a modest entry into the German market in 18 months.
>
> Our product has minor improvements compared with competitors (see Appendix X) which are protected by copyright and has been registered throughout the EC.

Most venture capitalists will seek confirmation of sales forecasts, either from past trading or they may want to speak to prospective customers. Be ready for this and provide as much supporting information as possible: market research data, published information, extracts from management accounts, customer lists, etc.

8. What do all those numbers mean?

There are several tendencies in business plans. Some people put in almost no numbers at all and don't outline their assumptions for those that they do include. Others put masses of numbers forward: five years of data, profit and loss accounts, balance sheets and cash flow forecasts. The mass of data is very seldom explained.

- What does it mean?
- Is this a good or a bad picture? Is it plausible?

One reason for the lack of clear explanation is that the writer has not thought this through. It is actually an essential discipline to think through what the numbers are saying. You must understand your own plan. Your first meeting with a potential financier is not the time to be confronted for the first time with, 'I see that you are forecasting a gradual decline in gross margins ... it doesn't seem to be explained by the changing sales mix ...'.

You are also telling a story and trying to tell it clearly and simply. Don't leave the reader of your work to spend hours of analysis and maybe come to the wrong conclusions. These conclusions may not be favourable to your case and you may not have the opportunity to explain.

Example

> The gross profit is forecast to decline gradually from an
> initial 60 per cent to around 35 per cent by year 4. This
> is largely due to the increase in sales through agents, at
> a lower margin, as explained in section 3. However, we
> have also allowed for a 5 per cent shrinkage in margins
> to combat competition as the market grows.

Try to show how sales and costs of sales are split by product. If
your business makes dusters and mops, for example, and they
have very different profitability, show how many units of each
you propose to sell and how much profit is expected to come from
each.

9. Sensitivity

'I received a business plan for a new venture from a businessman I respect. It was a freight business. I had wondered at the outset why he was looking for bank funding when he had the money to back it himself. The forecast showed a return to the shareholders of 500 per cent in the first year and 1000 per cent in the second. However, after careful reading, it appeared that if there was just 8 per cent less business than forecast then the enterprise would just break even, while a 15 per cent shortfall would mean a substantial loss and wipe out any bank loan.

Clearly, the risk reward ratio was fine for the shareholders but not for the financiers. I believe that by bringing out the sensitivity in the plan it would have been possible to address how the risk to the bank could be reduced and that there was indeed a way to do this that had been well thought through.'

Corporate finance adviser

A sensitivity analysis is just a calculation of what happens if. Typically it is based on sales not being as high as expected but it can also look at costs being higher, or indeed both of these problems occurring at once. It is usually best to start with an estimate of what fall in sales brings the project to break-even.

Why display the warts on the proposal in this way? Because the reader will certainly do it. If you have done the calculation yourself you are ready for the question. Your credibility will suffer if you have not calculated the risk. If you present the information yourself you prevent the reader getting the answer wrong (to your disadvantage). You also have the opportunity to say why the eventuality is very unlikely and how you would deal with the situation if it arose.

Often, costs that appear fixed can be cut if you have to. If trading is disastrous then staff can be laid off, although it might then take some time to staff up for recovery. Marketing costs that are essential for building a business can be cut if the sales are taking too long to respond. Growth may be sacrificed but survival may be ensured.

In the example given above the entrepreneur had a simple solution available. If sales did not meet target within four months he would close the company and a third-party guarantee would have ensured the bank did not lose any money. He should have set this out in his plan.

10. Check your assumptions – the reader will

Set out your important assumptions clearly and give some evidence to support them. It is important to make forecasts accessible to the reader. It is not enough that they are correct: the reader must be able to follow your thinking without needing a mainframe computer to recreate the process that arrived at the result.

> 'I recently received a nicely produced set of forecasts for a new business. The assumptions that had been used were scattered throughout the accompanying plan or were in the body of the forecast. The numbers in the cash flow were not always the same as those in the profit forecast and the two were not reconciled to each other. To cap it all, the forecast was printed out on a sheet 3 feet by 3 feet. While that did help to show three years' figures on one sheet of paper, it was not easy to use. It took me two hours to puzzle the whole thing out so it's just as well I was on their side.'
>
> *Corporate finance consultant*

Have a section dedicated to assumptions right by the forecast summary.

Example

---

1. Sales forecasts for the new business are based on 30 per cent of Oldco's sales; this is supported by existing clients who have said they will keep their business with the team, growing to 50 per cent by the end of the second year of trading, due to taking on four new clients (see marketing plan).
2. Pricing is set at a 5 per cent discount to Oldco's current level. It is felt that they will not respond by cutting prices but by trying to reinforce client loyalty.

Remember how important it is to think carefully about what assumptions we are making and to make them explicit.

Assumptions are the things we don't know we are making.

Explain important points

Example

---

1. Turnover fell in 1981 owing to the disruption caused by relocating. This was more than made up in the following year as growth resumed.
2. Gross profit has improved over the years and a target of 52 per cent is usual in the industry and will be achievable now that the company is large enough to buy in bulk and get volume discounts.

Particularly in start-ups, business promoters may be relying upon consultants' advice; do some checking of major assumptions, don't just rely on others.

'I received a business plan about a leisure business, seeking £750K, put together by property developers with the help of consultants who seemed inexperienced in this area. I rang several people in the industry, who were happy to discuss how it worked; two were major suppliers. I found out that the most important assumption in the plan, usage of the facility, was very optimistic. Three of the four industry people I spoke to thought the assumption unsafe.

This damaged the credibility of the forecasts. Why on earth didn't the promoters make a couple of telephone calls to double check their assumptions? They could have found out as quickly as I did.'

Corporate finance consultant

11. The famous dog leg forecast

You may feel that turnover and profits will rise dramatically as a result of your plans. If this follows years of trading on a lower track the reader probably won't believe you. Pause a moment and think about this. Look at the illustration below. Could you blame someone for having some doubts? Recheck your assumptions and your forecasts. Get someone independent to give you some impartial advice. Do they believe it? If you are certain, then go ahead but be sure that you have plausible arguments, *supported by evidence,* and not just by ambition; then try to persuade the reader.

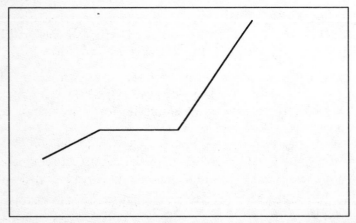

If you begin to have some doubts after re-examining your evidence don't be afraid to lower your forecasts.

> 'The chap said to me, "They don't want to see just OK growth, they want to see something impressive", so I told him, "Nobody is impressed by forecasts they don't believe".'
>
> *Corporate finance consultant*

You might be able to show that the business has been poorly managed and that the specific plans you have will increase sales. You must say what those plans are and why they should succeed. Merely employing more sales people is not enough. You must show that your product is competitive and that you can win market share, rather than spreading the same sales over more people.

You may be able to demonstrate a growing market for a new product you are introducing. Give some support for this if it is the case.

Whatever you do, don't show the famous dog leg without any supporting evidence.

Don't hide the dog leg by putting past trading in one bit of the document and the forecast elsewhere. That makes the document harder to read and irritates the reader but does not hide the information.

You may be worried that a financier will knock 15 per cent off your sales forecast, whatever you put down. You may well be right! The ways to combat this tendency are as follows:

1. Give good supporting evidence for your sales forecast. The more proof, the more likely they are to believe you.
2. Show the break-even of the business. Show a 'worst case' as well as your base case forecast.
3. Show your fixed and variable costs (get an accountant to help you if necessary) so that a reader can quickly compute what happens if sales are 15 per cent down on forecast.

It is often useful to show a best, middle and worst case. The worst case should truly be grim and show how you would deal with the situation. Don't simply show an optimistic, a more optimistic and a very optimistic outcome.

A last thought – a financier will certainly be put off by low profit expectations that do not show him a decent return. If this is a problem you are faced with remember that you have two choices:

1. Drop the project

2. Produce better returns, not by exaggeration but by rethinking how you can do things. Can you think of a way to run the business more profitably?

12. Why are you different?

It is quite surprising how few people state clearly why they should succeed. In a hard, competitive world businesses succeed because they have some competitive advantage. Maybe the management team is outstanding and has the track record to prove it. Maybe the product is new and exciting. Perhaps an extraordinarily good site has been secured. Perhaps the market is growing so fast that the suppliers cannot keep up.

Whatever the reasons are for you to succeed, write them clearly in your plan so that the reader doesn't have to search for reasons to back you. You will have said it so clearly, it couldn't be missed. Put these reasons in your summary also.

> 'This chap had a wonderful background. He was secretary of the industry's trade association. He had nearly 30 years' experience in the business with blue chip companies. He had just spent a year setting up businesses of just this type for a company. But he didn't make this really stand out. It was mentioned in passing and then you had to search through the appendices for his CV, sort of hidden. What a wasted opportunity!'
>
> *Venture capitalist*

Don't think that one major plus guarantees you backing. A sensible backer will ask, 'What is my risk, what can go wrong and what would my exposure be?' So give your reasons for success but *still* cover all the other key areas. So the market is growing at 80 per cent per annum. Say that but still provide evidence to convince the reader that *you* can take advantage of this, that you understand the supply, manufacture, selling, distribution and competition issues.

- How is your product or service different from one thousand competitors?
- What expertise or ideas do you have that will help you succeed?
- If your product does have advantages what are they?
- Can they be protected by copyright or patent?

Don't give vague generalisations; give some detail about these things.

Don't forget to talk about your competitors. Show you know who they are, have studied them, know how they are organised, what they are doing and know their strengths and weaknesses. Then say why you will beat them.

13. Tell me about your business

Your audience may know nothing about your business and industry; worse, they may think they do and be utterly mistaken. You must either educate the readers very quickly or put them right. Get the key facts over quickly and then come back with some more detail.

Briefly tell the reader what business or businesses you are in. This sets the scene. Answer the key questions that may occur but don't go into great detail at this stage.

- What does the business do?
- Where does it do it?
- How does it do it?
- Who does it sell its product or service to and how?
- Does it have key suppliers?
- How many outlets or factories does it have?
- How big is it? (turnover? profits? staff?)

Example

> Qualco is a family-owned and operated laundry and dry cleaning business. It has four shops located in Shepherd's Bush, Hammersmith, Holland Park and Putney. The shops each have a ZZZ dry cleaning machine but all laundry is sent to a central facility at Shepherd's Bush. The company's drivers have a daily round to each of the shops and also deliver and pick up from customers.

> Approximately 50 per cent of the business's £750,000 turnover is laundry and 80 per cent of that is contract work for some 70 hotels and restaurants in the West London area.

Explain how the business got to where it is. Clearly, this does not apply to a start-up proposal but would need to be replaced by more about the market and how you got involved. If the business has problems explain how they arose, what has been learned and how they will be or have been resolved. To understand a business and to believe forecasts it is important to see how the enterprise developed.

Example

LEEDS METROPOLITAN UNIVERSITY LIBRARY

> Sunblast was a loss-making business acquired by John Smith in 1987 for £100,000. He cut overheads, stopped dealing in low-volume products and brought it back to small profits before recruiting new management and becoming non-executive chairman. His new MD, Charles Jones, was an accountant, a former partner with Strutt & Grovel. Profits grew to £50,000 by 1990. In 1990 Jones persuaded Smith and the rest of the board to acquire Black Hole Ltd which was a complementary business. Unfortunately, it suffered a dramatic downturn in orders due to the insolvency of two major customers. Jones did not report this to the board for three months and sought to gain new customers rather than cutting overheads.
>
> Losses were £200,000 in 1991. The bank appointed a receiver and called on cross guarantees which put Sunblast in receivership although it was still trading profitably.

In this example, which is a proposal from a management buy-in team for funding to buy a company from a receiver, more explanation would be needed. A financier would need to be persuaded that the part of the business being bought was viable and that the problems that brought the group down really did not affect it.

For some businesses their regulation is a key aspect of the story. Regulations may not be at the kernel of operating a retail outlet, but for casinos, amusement machine hire, nursing homes, food distribution, road haulage, etc, they are.

> 'I have yet to see a financing proposal for a nursing home that simply and clearly explains relevant regulations, details the authorities who oversee their activities and explains how those authorities work.'
> *Consultant*

Dispel concerns. Your reader does not want to back a business that can be shut down at the whim of a far-off authority or as a result of a small error. Explain clearly how it all works and how your internal control ensures you do not fall foul of the authorities.

14. Your market and competitors

This aspect of the business is partly covered in other sections but it also warrants its own separate mention. The three crucial areas of any business are the product, the management and *the market*. Everything else is detail.

> 'I was doing some strategy work with a very impressive small firm of accountants. They openly avowed that they knew very little of what their competitors were doing. It is true that information is hard to come by in that market but professionals are slow to see themselves as competing in just the way that any business does. Research is often easier than you think. It is usually easy to get firms' brochures. That on its own tells one a lot. Apart from knowing how they are fighting you, if you know who is doing what, you can copy the best ideas.'
>
> *Strategy consultant*

It is amazing how many plans seem to describe businesses without competitors. Even if there are some acknowledged competitors they are usually blighted by having inferior products. At the risk of sounding pompous, just because a competitor has an inferior product that does not mean that you will beat them in the struggle in the market-place. Many people felt that Sony's Betamax video recording system was technically superior to the VHS system that triumphed. The European Community will license one system of high definition TV. That may be one that is technically the best but it may also be one that is produced by a European rather than a Japanese company.

Issues such as distribution, pricing, packaging and promotion as well as the strength of competitors are the determinants of success. It is essential to set out these issues, possibly briefly, in a business plan. A potential backer's confidence is boosted by the perception that you know your competitors and customers.

The customer is the second ingredient missing from many business plans. Who are yours? If you know that you serve primarily C1/C2 males aged between 18 and 30 then do say so. You build confidence that you know what you are doing, disarm potential questions and it allows you to say that your market is stable, growing, has high disposable income, etc. Your market may be primarily supermarket buyers and only secondarily the end-user. You need to get on to the shelves before you can worry about competing for the consumer's pound. Talk about your immediate market – the buyers – but don't ignore the end-user. If they don't buy from the shelves then the supermarket buyers will not reorder.

- What trends are observable in your market?
- What changes can occur?

> 'My client produced a system to protect sunbathers from ultraviolet radiation. It worked on UVA radiation which has a shorter wavelength. Then newspaper reports started stressing the importance also of longer wavelength UVB. The issue was not the technical effectiveness but producing an effective marketing response to maintain customer confidence.'
>
> *Corporate finance consultant*

Some changes can be anticipated. The reader of a business plan is likely to want to know what might happen, however speculative. Again, by raising issues you can disarm them before they develop into a negative aura around your project.

None of this need take an enormous effort nor need it result in a 200-page document. A comment, a paragraph, and each issue is addressed.

15. Don't forget to tell them why you are there

Another strange thing about business plans is that people often devote enormous energy to writing them and then don't ask for what they need.

This is a bit like the salesman who charms the customers and has them begging to buy and then doesn't tell them what is for sale or what it costs. Can you imagine Prince Charming forgetting to ask Sleeping Beauty to marry him?

There should be a section in every business plan devoted to expressing the size and duration of the need and asking for the money. Some people are sure what terms they will offer to investors and can tell the reader precisely what is on offer. This sometimes invites a yes or no response when there may be scope for discussion and negotiation, so be cautious about doing this. As a rule your forecasts should end at the trading profit line (after all expenses except for interest); leave the financiers to deal with the financial structure and what interest rate to apply.

If you know that you need £300,000 plus a three-year bank guarantee for £200,000 then say so. It is not necessary to work out the precise deal: the split between equity and debt and the precise terms. You are bound to meet someone who wants to do it differently. You may even be offering better terms than you need to. Leave it flexible for discussions.

It is not easy to go back and ask for more cash a few months after a financier has invested. Don't pare your estimates to the bone and ask for too little. On the other hand, don't ask for what is clearly more than you need; this harms your credibility. Allow a sufficient contingency for the business going better than expected as well as worse: expansion costs money too.

Repeat your need in the summary at the beginning of your business plan. Make sure the reader has not turned the first page before knowing what you want and what will justify their support.

Example

The cash forecast shows a maximum cash need of £580,000 six months after opening. Delayed payments for capital expenditure are the key to this and have been negotiated. Allowing for a 10 per cent contingency on usage, which is already conservative, the investment requirement is £750,000. This can be financed as follows:

Promoters	£200,000
Trade investor	£100,000
Brewery loan	£150,000
	£450,000
Funding gap	£300,000
Total financial requirement	£750,000

The business is forecast to be cash positive from opening and the payback period is 3.5 years.

16. How much are you investing?

An entrepreneur or manager has many ways to show commitment but none is as persuasive as money. If a wealthy individual is promoting what is claimed to be an exciting business but is not prepared to put up a substantial investment, that is a big cause of worry to backers.

If someone proves they have invested everything in getting a project thus far then one has sympathy. It is important to state how much the promoters are investing. If it is past expenditure give details of cash invested. If it is an investment in time justify a value for that time. Investors frequently ask for a statement of affairs and will expect you to borrow to put some cash up alongside them.

Why do investors think like this? If the going gets tough and the business has to struggle through, the investor wants to be convinced that you will stick with it and devote your total energy to protecting both of your investments. It must be hard for you to walk away.

> Of a proposal to raise funding for a bowling centre ...
> 'The money to be invested by the shareholders is too small (£300,000 on a £1,500,000 project) ... it doesn't show commitment ... anyway, they all own companies that will do work for the new company and they are charging fees that will recover their money within a year ... we're taking all the risk!'
>
> *Leasing company executive*

It is never very impressive when someone wants investment and you find out that they are proposing to charge fees to the business through another company they own. It may be perfectly proper but it does make one feel uneasy. Always state and justify such plans clearly. The shareholders' agreement may well forbid such connected transactions.

People also often seek unreasonable rewards from the business either through large salaries, before the business has proved itself, or through a very large shareholding. Entrepreneurs will often say they want to invest as little as possible in a scheme, yet when asked what share of the business they want to retain they make excessive demands. Take professional advice on what is achievable. Don't seek an excessive salary if you want outside investment and don't even state what share of the business is available to investors. That way you don't alienate potential investors before even meeting them.

It is surprising how many business plans don't state that a substantial investment will be put in by the promoter of the enterprise or that funds have already been raised towards the total requirement. Confidence rises dramatically when it is revealed. But if it is left unsaid in the document then the financier may never pick up the phone and give you the opportunity to say it. If money is raised after the document is written, either rewrite the document or add a covering letter.

Avoid showing balance sheets like this:

Intangible Assets £500,000   Shareholders' Funds   £500,000

If time, effort, patents and expertise are being valued, explain and justify that valuation. Note that an investor may not agree with you.

This expertise that you are valuing is only worth what someone will pay for it or what it will earn. A financier may need persuading of this value. You can demonstrate earning power *after* you get the finance but not before, while you may only be able to sell the business or business idea after you demonstrate earning power.

17. Why you shouldn't lie

Most people have incidents in their careers that could be embarrassing. Things not to be proud of, mistakes that have been made, things that might be misinterpreted – even where one was totally in the right. There are also things management know about their businesses that may not find favour with superiors or business partners. It is not our duty in preparing a business plan to advertise the warts on a situation, *as long as we are not dishonest in hiding them.*

It is sensible to try to portray ourselves and our companies in the best possible light. We can be very creative when we describe things: exaggerating our part in a triumph, omitting to mention failure that can decently be ignored, using language to build an impression of excellence. That is all part of the game and entirely reasonable. Where problems are created is in the downright lie or, just as bad, the blatant misrepresentation.

Sometimes people only try to delay the moment of reckoning. They may forget to mention the outstanding litigation, hoping that when it comes out the other party will be too committed to withdraw. It is always worth considering that obvious attempts to mislead strike at *trust*. If our business partner or superior stops trusting us the likelihood of a deal or a *successful* deal diminishes. It is hard to run a company when superiors or financiers always seek confirmation of all information and also refuse all non-essential funding.

- Where is the line between being dishonest and 'let the buyer beware'?
- What if nobody ever finds out?

No buyer of a business expects a seller to reveal that a competitor is about to launch a devastating new product. However, a venture capitalist financing a business would. Most people know which side of the line they are walking.

No book like this can predict whether someone will be caught, but never underestimate the consequences. Investors have legal remedies against directors (personally) who are party to misrepresentation: they can also be extremely awkward, just when their support is most needed, if they do not trust their partner. Do not assume that the investor will always simply follow clear financial self-interest and stick with a deal with someone they don't trust. They may feel it is cheaper not to throw good money after bad.

'I sacrificed £75,000 of legal and accountancy costs we had incurred by pulling out of a deal at the last minute when I discovered that I didn't trust the MD I was backing. The chap had only held back a bit about previous liquidations with which he had been involved but it was clearly material information. Better to lose some money now than the whole investment later.'

Venture capitalist

'I was trying to raise money for a group of people promoting a project. One of my partners had had business dealings with one of them before and rated him highly. After a few days this man told me over the phone that he had been foolish. In order to avoid scaring off potential investors with the size of the project he had only revealed half the price being paid for the business. The balance was actually available from his colleagues who were investing far more than he had revealed. While the project now appeared more attractive in a purely financial sense, we wouldn't touch it with a barge pole. If he'd lie once he'd lie again. He could harm us and our reputation. So we stopped work. I have no idea whether he ever raised the money.'

Independent financial adviser

18. Don't sell your story by the kilo – use appendices

Business plans can get pretty thick with your supporting evidence incorporated. They can also get a bit confusing, not to say hard to read if the text is one hundred pages long. Remember you are telling a story. Tell your story with the key points and summary evidence and put the supporting data in appendices at the end. You may want to have this as a separate document so that the task of reviewing your plan does not appear too daunting.

The sort of evidence should be:

- Detailed CVs of the key managers
- Detailed forecasts
- Press cuttings
- Brochures
- Market survey data
- Reports by industry experts
- Map of site locations
- Sales data by customer, eg key customer analysis
- List of competitive products
- Information on competitors
- Product costing data
- Property valuations, details of leases
- Plans of important buildings, eg for hotel project give some idea of the building
- Details of patents and technical specifications
- Major contractual agreements
- Detailed staffing information

- Audited accounts.

Don't throw in the kitchen sink, only put in relevant, helpful and usable information.

> 'The business plan had, as an appendix, all the firm's monthly newsletters to their sales agents (about 15 pages). They added some background colour but they were not relevant to the investment decision. I'll judge a deal by whether the firm's products are selling, not by whether they keep in touch with their salesforce.'
>
> *Venture capitalist*

Be selective; don't make your reader plough through unnecessary paper. That can be irritating; you do not want to have that effect.

19. Timing: Don't leave it so late!

First (and only) Law of Timing

Everything always takes longer than you expect.

Example

> You need someone to do something urgently but they are out, then they are busy on something else; they have other clients. They can't find the file, then they respond but you are out so they post it. It misses the post and is delayed for a day. The post takes two days and not one. You are out on the day it arrives. You reply at once but need further information, losing a day, then your typist is sick so a day is lost; then the franking machine seizes up at 5 pm and you lose another day, etc.

Sensible investors will not allow themselves to be rushed into putting money into a venture without having the opportunity to investigate it properly and to think about it. You must give the investor time. Even if the venture you propose is extremely attractive and easy to investigate it will take *at least* four weeks from the first meeting to get cash. The legal stages will take that time. Eight weeks is a more reasonable assessment. Many private investors explain that they make decisions quickly while financial institutions are slow. Our experience is that private investors are no quicker.

Many businesses or projects are set up, perhaps in order to prove the idea *before* seeking finance, and then finance is sought against the background of a ticking clock. Money is being spent on overheads but the launch cannot go ahead without more funding. The launch itself may be tied to a trade show or a 'buying season'. You are in a hurry: you are committed. You are losing money with every day of delay; or time – if the season is missed you may have to wait until next year to launch. The investor is suspicious, 'We are being rushed, what are they trying to hide?'

> 'If they want an answer immediately then it is no.'
> *Venture capitalist*

Start getting your finance arranged in plenty of time. Very few of the people who are in such a hurry couldn't have started looking months earlier.

> 'I met the directors of a very exciting young company who needed working capital to help establish the business. They were in discussions with a potential investor who was messing them around but they decided to exhaust the possibility before coming back to me. They rang up about three months later because they were desperate and needed cash within two weeks because their bank was just about to appoint a receiver. In three months one can do something, not in two weeks.'
>
> *Venture capitalist*

A final point to remember is that if you are desperate then you are in a very weak negotiating position.

20. Presentation is not all

On the other hand, presentation is not negligible. If a document is badly typed and looks a mess it does not create an aura of professionalism or of confidence. A very poor presentation is one of the quickest means to consign a business plan to a waste bin.

A two-page handwritten note faxed to a financial institution may win finance for a project. The point of this book is to advise on *maximising your chances*. You will do that if you present an impressive document.

> 'A client of mine had adjusted his plan for the umpteenth time before sending it to an institution he had not tried before. Then something happened and he had further changes. He decided to explain these in a covering letter. I told him, "You may be wasting your time to change the plan yet again but, *if I were you,* I'd invest the effort. It may only add 5 per cent to your chances but you've come this far …"'
> *Accountant with many small business clients*

The document should be produced on good quality paper, using a good quality printer. It should be typed and bound. If appendices are included use page separators; make sure that they are well photocopied if they are copies. Spend money.

However, there is another contrary illusion that some people suffer from. They think that a beautiful document will produce the necessary backing. If a plan does not add up for some reason, it has a gap or unanswered questions or an error and yet the reader sees a beautiful document it raises the question of whether the writer is simply trying to create an illusion.

The other problem is that you can direct scarce time and energy in the wrong direction. In the final analysis it is the substance of a plan that persuades someone to back it. A reasonable appearance is only one necessary stage to getting it read; once read it must make sense.

21. 'Everyone asks for something different'

It is a mistake to miss out important issues just because readers adopt different angles on a project. *That way you have it wrong for everybody!*

> 'One client had no business plan at all on the grounds that everyone asks for something different, so why bother with a standard document. However, he was effectively producing dozens of plans; one for each investor. One standard business plan would have suited them all and they could have asked for any additional information they wanted. He wasted an enormous amount of time. He also wasted money because we had to write a summary for him to send out and for which he was charged.'
>
> *Corporate finance consultant*

If you tell your story clearly and put in the supporting data or refer to it then you should answer all the questions. So you miss out something or someone has a weird approach to the project that is different from everyone else and you have to send some follow-up information: that is not as time-consuming as having to produce something different for everyone; a different plan for each recipient. Remember that delay is lost money and lost opportunity.

Saying that everyone asks for something different, which is why things have been left out, is an excuse for having produced a poor business plan. If you follow the advice set out in this document and if you explain your business, your market, your team, your forecasts and your proposals clearly, then you will not need to offer that excuse. You will have covered all the issues anyone may ask about.

You only get one chance

If your plan does not convince then there is seldom any point going back with amendments.

> 'A client had a two-page plan drawn up by a consultant and sent out to venture capitalists. Some months later the plan was completely rethought and we helped to rewrite it as a much fuller document. However, when this was sent to organisations which had received the previous version they said they had turned down the proposal and would not reopen it.'
>
> *Corporate finance consultant*

A bad first impression is very hard to shift.

If you have to revise the figures in a plan then it is better to do that than to let the reader spot errors. However, revisions do not inspire confidence.

It is true that some venture capital institutions use checklists and that not all of these are the same. It is also true that occasionally one will be so excited by meeting you that they will virtually write your plan for you at the same time as they write their proposal to their credit committee. However, it is very rare for anyone to raise money successfully without a proper business plan, so at least improve your chances. Even if you turned out not to need the plan or needed to redraft it, merely having written it in the first place ought to have improved your presentation and your ability to present your case out of all recognition.

22. How big? How fast?

You face a dilemma when you have to choose how big to start a business and how fast you want it to grow.

It is more difficult to get funding for a small project than for a big one. There is a host of reasons:

- The financier thinks that it is more difficult to sell a one-unit business, for example, than one with several outlets. Therefore, it will be harder for him to get his money out of the smaller business.
- It is as much work to complete and then monitor a small deal as a large one.
- If a financier has a target of how much money he needs to invest he may prefer to do three big deals than 15 small ones.
- A bigger business can afford more management and more financial control and therefore provide more information for the investor.

The investor also wants a high rate of return to compensate for the investments that don't pay off. To achieve this an annual rate of return is set at around 30 to 40 per cent. To achieve such a high return the investor needs a business to grow fast and then to be sold within five to seven years. Not all venture capital funds work in this way, but most do.

As a businessman how do you deal with these pressures?

If your deal is a small, single site business, don't try to create a bigger business just to accommodate the financier. It won't be convincing. Think through your alternatives for financing a small business. These include funding from relatives, friends, private investors or firms, factoring, and bank finance. If you need to raise your own funds consider whether remortgaging your house or raising money on endowment policies or on your pension scheme are options you wish to pursue. Before pursuing these routes always think very carefully about the risks involved and take professional advice. Remember that if your business fails you could lose your house and your pension too.

However, if you are starting small but have a *clear plan for growth* then *put this in your plan*. Explain clearly how you will grow, over what time, how you will compete and why you should succeed. Put forward your growth strategy that will excite investors.

Remember, though, that this should not just be a vague wish list; provide the evidence to convince the reader that you are serious, that you have thought this through and that you will succeed. Give numbers, show you have the management resources and that the opportunity really exists. Plans that give vague, unsupported and unrealistic expansion schemes, completed, as often as not by a statement such as, 'Our objective is a stock market quotation in three to four years', are a real turn off!'

Example

> The current proposal is for a single-site operation. Once that is well established, which we believe will take nine months, the development strategy is to add one new site every six to nine months. As set out in the section on marketing above, there are many towns with a clear potential for one of our units. We propose to create a regional group by expansion in south-west England and the southern Midlands. Details of targeted towns are given in Appendix X. Our initial target is for eight to nine units within five years which would be expected to yield £3 million trading profit and have a peak cash requirement of £6 million.

> Once the first site has been open for three months Jim
> Bond will spend 30 per cent of his time developing new
> projects. After six to nine months Peter Speed will be
> able to devote a like proportion of his time. A small
> head office will be set up within the first unit and the
> proven accounting systems to be installed there will be
> easily adapted to suit all the units.
>
> Appendix XI shows the projected cash needs and
> returns for this development plan.

Rapid growth places enormous strains on management to put
systems in place to control it and financiers know that:

> The accounts department can't send out all the
> invoices as quickly as usual so customers don't pay.
> The computer can't cope with the number of entries
> going through and keeps on 'crashing'. Staff are busy
> on other things so management accounts aren't
> produced regularly. The owners are busy dealing with
> customers so someone in the warehouse takes
> advantage of the lack of supervision and starts stealing
> stock. There is no time to train staff so they need extra
> supervision. Debtors are stretching, margins are falling,
> nobody knows what is going on and sales keep
> growing . . . panic reigns.

It is no accident that many of the fastest growing companies
collapse. If you plan growth of more than 25 per cent per annum
explain clearly how you will control it. If you plan 100 per cent
or more expect concern, and explain in considerable detail how
you will control this growth.

23. Cash, cash, cash

Your business plan may show a fabulous profit projection but if you run out of cash you will never achieve it.

Cash is a simple idea. You can tell from your bank balance whether you can pay a bill. Profit is a more slippery idea. Of course, it is the surplus of income over expenditure over a defined period. That sounds simple. But accountants may, under certain circumstances, allow a company to take in the income from a deal that was not finalised until *after* the year end. They may allow certain expenses to be treated as the purchase of an asset. For instance, the salaries of a property department are, in big companies, often added to the value of properties bought in the year. They don't appear in the profit and loss account. And depreciation ...

Growing businesses usually require cash to fund bigger stocks, higher debtors and more staff. Profits are seldom high enough to provide all this cash, so even while you are making good profits you may need to go to the bank for more money. This is a critical stage for your business and one where, if the bank says no, you have a major problem.

At an early stage in the development of a business you may have heavy start-up costs or initial losses. You may find that progress is slower than you expected. Again, a profitable business may run out of cash.

To deal with cash there are several things you can do.

- Any business plan should include a cash flow forecast.
  This should be broken down into months and show quite a lot of detail, not just an income line and an expenses line.
- You should do some 'what-if' scenarios in your plan.
  Prove that you can survive an economy in recession, orders taking longer to come through or business not achieving your target.

Don't fund opening losses with bank borrowing unless you really have no option. The setting-up costs of a business should be financed with equity capital.

> 'We have come across many businesses which started with an overdraft and not enough capital. Often they run into a problem. Perhaps the banks says "enough" before the business has turned the corner. Maybe the manager says "no more" just as the business starts to grow and needs cash for expansion. Don't blame the banks; they have no duty to take risks, they are in business too; it is the entrepreneur who has used the wrong sort of funding.'
>
> *Accountant*

Bank managers and financiers share the characteristic that they don't like nasty surprises. Try to deal with problems in the business plan so you can demonstrate that this is not a surprise. It is often a good idea to talk about financial control in the business plan. Worse than a nasty surprise for your financier is one which you did not know was coming yourself, and even worse than that is not being able to show that you know your current financial position. All this can only be dealt with by having an adequate accounting system for a business of your size and type. Most businesses that fail also have a breakdown in their financial control and information systems.

A final thought on cash is that investors also want cash out of a business; maybe not at once but eventually.

'Post-production businesses typically make good profits, all of which they have to continually reinvest in bigger and better state-of-the-art equipment. The technology is continually improving and all the competitors are buying the latest equipment. You never see any cash *out* of those businesses. No thanks, it's not for me.'

Venture capitalist

24. The five-year forecast

Five-year forecasts are very useful. They are useful for scrap paper, for making paper darts and for rolling into little balls to throw into the bin on dull days.

To be fair, in some industries there *is* some hope of a forecast being half way accurate so far in the future. Certainly a forecast as such is always useful to show the direction one will take and what the outcome will be if everything goes according to plan. Indeed, the financier wants to see how much money might be made if everything works out. So the presence of a forecast in a business plan is not at issue. The important point is to maintain credibility and to make life easy for the reader.

Present this forecast information by having a section which shows a summary of the forecasts for one to three years: five years only if there is a good reason. Such a good reason might be a believable plan to float the company in five years, or to demonstrate how debt could be repaid in five years. It is better to show a convincing, and impressive, two- or three-year outlook than a mass of numbers that nobody believes.

Always put the summary of past trading together with the forecast. *Don't* make the reader search through the document to compare past and future. *Don't* put the past and future in different formats, even if things change: the reader immediately wonders what you are hiding by making it hard to compare.

Example

	Actual	—Forecast—		
Year	1	2	3	4
Sales £000				
product 1	100	120	130	130
product 2	0	0	20	30
	100	120	150	160
Gross profit £000				
product 1	20	20	25	30
product 2 ·	0	0	5	10
	20	20	30	40

Put detailed figures, for two years, in appendices. Nobody believes detailed expense analyses forecast five years ahead. If someone really wants such detail then it can be produced on request.
Naturally, the summary must be believable. If key ratios (such as
overheads/sales) vary significantly from one year to another explain why.

Treat the forecast as a tool for showing what will happen and
why. Explain why the numbers turn out the way they do; don't
force the reader to plough through detail. If there is a message
spell it out. The forecast is just the evidence for the message.

Example

> The forecast demonstrates how profits will rise rapidly
> as turnover increases. This is because overheads will
> not increase as fast as turnover. The reasons for this
> are set out in Section ...

25. Danger: Prospectuses and how to avoid them

If you write a business plan that goes beyond describing the business and invites the reader to invest *take care!*

In order to protect the general public from fraudulent or merely misleading invitations to invest, the law sets down safeguards for the form of offers to the public. If you invite investment from more than about 40 or 50 people, other than family and personal acquaintances, your document is likely to be a prospectus.

Why does this matter?

The requirements for a prospectus include items which will cost the issuer money, eg an accountant's report. Furthermore, there is a general requirement not to issue a misleading document. In a business plan you can inform a potential investor that you have done your best to ensure that information is accurate but they must make their own enquiries to confirm key points. That is not good enough for a prospectus. If your document is a prospectus and proves misleading, an investor who loses money can sue you personally to make it good. Issuing a prospectus that does not comply with the law is also a criminal offence.

Merely checking your document and ensuring that each phrase and claim can be supported by evidence is hard work. You will probably need professional help (more expense) and the document becomes increasingly bland and dull as you cut out your phrases which are true but hard to prove.

'Before sending out a document to potential investors I go through it line by line and highlight each claim or statement of fact. I then get written evidence for each one and file them with a cross reference to the document. This would include published data, newspaper reports, company accounts etc. If relying upon the opinion of a director then the document must say "In the directors' opinion" or "The directors believe" but they must still have some reasonable grounds for that belief. I then write down all these beliefs and get them to sign, taking resposibility for them. It certainly focuses their minds.'
Corporate finance executive with a firm of accountants

What should you do to avoid expense and risk?

1. You need have no concern if you are sending documents only to banks and financial institutions. None of the following need apply then. However, if you send documents to accountants or financial intermediaries and they may pass them on (because you haven't asked them not to) you must assume your document is a prospectus.
2. Number each document you send out and send no more than 40. Instruct the recipient (in the document) not to pass it on to anyone else.
3. Make it clear on the front cover that the document is a business plan or information memorandum and not an invitation to invest. Actually *say* that the potential investor should take professional advice and is expected to make further enquiries, that the document is only intended to arouse interest to pursue the matter further.
4. Don't set out a clear scheme with so many shares available at so much per share. Don't include a subscription form.

Of course, accuracy should be a concern of anyone who produces a business plan even if it isn't a prospectus. Investors who lose money try to find someone to sue for its recovery. Venture capital institutions will conduct their own investigations but you cannot be sure that a private investor will. If someone is relying on your document go through it with care.

Appendix 1
Checklist: What has to be in a business plan?

Not everything on this checklist needs to be in a plan for every business but you should mark the ones you have omitted and be sure there is a good reason for their omission.

You may want to put things in a different order or under different headings. It is only important that the information is there and the story flows logically.

Front page
  Title
  Date document was produced
  Contacts for further information

Summary

Index

Introduction

Background to proposal

History of business *(or previous relevant businesses)*

Outline of the business
  The product service
    what it is, what it does, how it is special, *(unique selling proposition)*
  The market

size, growth, trends
customers *(who they are, why they will buy from you)*
    any key customers accounting for a high proportion of the
    business?
competitors *(who, market share, strengths and weaknesses,
market segmentation, pricing)*
Sourcing
    use of sub-contractors
    any key suppliers you are dependent upon?
Manufacturing processes
    patents, copyrights etc
Sales and distribution
Premises and plant.

Trading summary
The past trading *(if any)*
Forecasts
Assumptions
Explanation of key points
Seasonality
Minimum information:
    turnover
    gross profit
    overheads
    profit before interest and tax
Balance sheet
Cash flow forecast
    monthly cash position *(if there is a mid-month low it may be
    material to funding needs)* working capital/number of days
    of stock, etc.

Management
Background of key managers *(including achievements and ex-
perience in similar businesses)*
Organisation structure
    staffing levels and skills
Shareholdings/investment

The proposal
Amount to be raised *(amount contributed by you)*
How it is to be used

Existing bankers/financiers *(facilities, amounts advanced, security)*

Strategy
  Where your business is going
  How you will get it there
  Why you are different

Risk
  Areas of risk, what happens if, break-even

Appendices
  Illustration and support for the plan.

Appendix 2
Cash flow forecasts: A guideline

These mysterious things are demanded for most business enterprises. Why? Because businesses fail for only one reason: if they run out of cash. A profitable business can fail while an unprofitable business can survive. This is because profits are created by accountants while cash is produced by businesses.

Example

> The profitable business sells more goods than it can really finance. The creditors demand payment but the customers are delaying payment. They will pay. They do pay. But they are too late. The creditors stopped supplying ... the bank appointed a receiver ... and the cheque arrived too late. Yet the business always made healthy profits.
>
> The unprofitable business produces accounts which show losses year after year. Yet the sales continue to grow and eventually they reach a level where profits are recorded. How is this possible? Maybe the losses are due to a high depreciation charge. The depreciation expense shown in the accounts does not reflect cash going out of the business. It is a measure of the diminishing value of and need to replace assets. Maybe the suppliers continue to extend larger and larger credit.

Cash forecasts are not that hard to do

You may need some help from an accountant to check your forecast but there is no reason why anyone in business cannot draft their own.

What is a cash forecast?

It is a statement of the cash flows into and out of the business. If your business had just one bank account and all payments to you and by you went through this then the cash flow would be a listing of these payments.

Monthly or weekly?

Most cash flows are produced in monthly periods because it is a lot more work, obviously, to do it in weekly periods. There may, however, be occasions where a business may have a satisfactory bank balance at the beginning and the end of a month but have a serious overdraft in the middle. The monthly cash flow forecast would give no indication of this problem. Do not ignore it. Whoever you send the business plan to will feel seriously misled if they find that you actually need a lot more cash than you have disclosed. It is no comfort to them to hear that this is a very short-term problem.

The fact is that you will need extra cash or bank facilities. Either show a weekly cash forecast, if the problem is a recurring one, or flag it prominently in the text and explain it, if it is a 'one off'.

Timing

Don't start the cash forecast unrealistically soon. If you are seeking start-up finance in June and your forecast assumes the business will start trading in July then you are probably not being realistic. It is very common to be given a document that was prepared some time previously. Unfortunately, there is no alternative, you must update it. Unless a business really isn't affected by seasons it is misleading to show a start in February when it is already May!

> 'I was shown a very interesting plan for a new hotel, due to open in February. Unfortunately, it was already February, financing had taken longer than anticipated and, on the best assumptions, it would be impossible to open before June. The summer season would therefore be missed. The cash flow forecast had not been altered and was therefore materially wrong. The cash needs for the business would be far higher than anticipated because there would be no summer profits to build the bank balance up before the loss-making winter period set in.'
>
> *Hotel consultant*

Consistency

Check that the assumptions in the cash forecast are the same as in your profit forecast. It is not unknown for different versions of a plan to get mixed up and for the figures to be contradictory.

Always check that your figures are consistent. Errors will be spotted and will hit your credibility badly.

Optimism

While optimism is a good characteristic it must be reasonable. Don't show orders coming in earlier than they really will. Don't show customers paying before they really will. Remember that new businesses are often asked to pay in advance or are given very little credit.

Seasonality

Remember that some months are better than others. Allow for holiday months. Allow for some months having more trading days than others.

VAT

Don't forget that with VAT you collect tax for the government and pay it over, on average, some 10 weeks later. Of course, you also pay VAT on your purchases and expenses. However, on balance VAT will probably help you to finance your business. Don't leave it out of the calculations. It is best to show sales and purchases excluding VAT and show three extra lines:

VAT collected on sales	monthly
VAT paid on purchases	monthly
VAT re-/payments from/to Customs & Excise	usually quarterly.

Timing of PAYE etc

Some payments, PAYE is a good case, are made later than the expense they are associated with. Don't forget to show the delay.

Interest

Don't assume how the business will be financed and show the interest on the level of debt you assume. The outcome will be different. Only show interest on, say, the trading overdraft of the business.

Stocks

If stocks are to be built up or worked down during the period shown it is worth showing opening and closing levels. Remember:

Opening stocks + Purchases - Cost of sales - Stock losses
= Closing stock

Bank facilities

If the cash forecast shows a need for borrowing it is worth stating what bank facilities are in place. If there is a need greater than the availability address the issue. How will it be dealt with?

> '... the cash forecast showed a large and growing overdraft for a new publishing company. In fact, this was money being used to set up and develop the business and not an overdraft, which should be for short-term needs. It was the basic capital needed by the business. There was no security for a bank and none, in my experience, would advance money in the particular circumstances. This particular line in the forecast represented a "hole" which needed filling. By not addressing how it would be filled, it gave a bad impression when the forecast was sent to the bank, which had no intention of filling it.'
>
> *Corporate finance adviser*

The following example gives an idea of how to lay out a cash forecast and some of the categories of expense that should go in it. It is not exhaustive. Every business is different and it is important to think through what you spend money on and to put that category in the cash flow.

Do your best to put expenses and receipts in the right months.

	January	**February** etc

Cash from sales

Purchases

Wages
National Insurance
PAYE
Pension scheme
Health insurance
Staff recruitment
Rent
Rates
Service charge
Advertising and PR
Insurance
Motor expenses
Electricity
Telephone

Stationery
Postage
Audit and accountancy
Legal and professional
Travel
Entertainment
Sundry

VAT

Leases/HP etc
Interest and bank charges

Cash inflow/(outflow)

Opening bank balance
Closing bank balance

Glossary

Balance sheet A statement of the assets and liabilities of a business at a point in time.

Break-even The state of a business where it is making no profit and no loss. It is employed as a means of showing how low sales need to get or how poor margins need to be before the business reaches this state. There are other variables that might be tested in this way, for example business X will trade at break-even if wage costs rise 7 per cent.

Cash flow Quite literally, the cash that goes into and out of a business. See Appendix 2.

Creditor Someone to whom you owe money.

CV Short for curriculum vitae. A biographical sketch, literally the course of one's life. A statement of someone's background; what schools, colleges or universities they went to, what qualifications they achieved, what jobs they have had.

Debtor Someone who owes you money.

Depreciation Accountants charge as a business expense the declining value of an asset as it gets older. This originated, sensibly enough, as a means of ensuring that people recognised the hidden cost of the wasting away in value of, say, a machine used in a business. So if it had a five-year life the original cost would be charged as an expense over five years. Complications set in with inflation and property values going up and not down as they got older. Life got more difficult with the tax authorities calculating depreciation for their purposes differently from methods used in most accounts. Don't worry about it.

Entrepreneur Someone who undertakes an enterprise. Used colloquially to describe a business person who is prepared to take risks (with their own and other people's money) in anticipation of financial reward if their enterprise is successful.

Financial accounts Financial accounts are the figures, after amending management accounts, presented to shareholders, tax authorities and bankers in order to convey what managers want them to believe about how the business is doing.

Gross profit Income from sales of a product or service less the costs directly associated with getting it in a state to sell. So the cost of materials used in manufacture and factory labour are deducted. However, for a bowling centre, for instance, the staff costs are not deducted because they are there whether or not the service is sold. They are therefore not a direct cost.

Guarantee Often a controlling shareholder of a business will be asked to give a personal guarantee to a bank that they will personally repay debts to it if their business cannot pay. Companies can similarly give guarantees. Banks can be asked to give guarantees on behalf of companies, for example a performance guarantee provides compensation to a customer if a contract is not fulfilled.

Intangible assets A business may have an asset such as know-how, which cannot be seen or touched but can be sold and therefore has a value. While this value can be put in a balance sheet, investors are often sceptical about how the value was arrived at.

K 1000, derived from kilo. As in £10K.

Management accounts Produced weekly, monthly or quarterly, these are the figures that managers use to tell them where they are and how their business is doing. They are different from financial accounts which are presented in ways prescribed by law.

Margin Usually expressed as a percentage. The sales value less the costs of a product or service, divided by the sales value.

Market share A percentage (usually by value) of a defined market, for example the market for plastic buckets in the UK. Remember that there may be segments of it, such as children's toys, household, builders' buckets, etc.

Ordinary shares Also A and B ordinary shares, preference shares and debentures. Don't worry about them.

A company is initially funded in two ways: by borrowing from a bank or through its share capital. The shareholders own the company and divide their investment into so many shares and they assign a notional value to each. For example, they invest £10,000 in 10,000 shares, each of which has a value of £1. There can be different types of share that can have different rights to income, profits, the value of the business, votes, etc.

Overheads Business expenses not directly related to producing a product or service.

Pre-opening costs The costs such as legal, survey, architects' fees, etc which are incurred before opening a business unit but which are usually added to its capital cost.

Profit The surplus of income over expenses over a defined period. However, there are so many ways of manipulating this apparently simple concept, particularly in larger businesses, that profit is a deceptively simple idea.

Profit and loss account A statement of the income and expenses of a business over a defined period. It is different from a cash flow in two ways; it counts income and expenses that relate to that period, even if the cash did not come in or go out in it, and it counts non-cash expenses such as depreciation.

Receiver When a bank lends and takes security it gets the borrower to agree that if the payments are not met on time a receiver can be appointed. This person takes charge of the business from management, sells the security, repays the lender and gives whatever is left back to the owners. Often what is left cannot carry on trading and a liquidator is appointed, who sells off whatever is left to pay suppliers, staff, tax authorities, etc.

Rights issue Companies may raise money by offering their existing shareholders the 'right' to invest more money for more shares. They will be offered so many new shares at such-and-such a price for each share they currently own. Companies that are quoted on the London Stock Exchange are obliged to offer their existing shareholders the first right to buy new shares. However, there are ways around this, such as by buying another company in exchange for issuing new shares to the sellers.

Security (for a loan) Assets which are pledged to a bank so that if a business cannot meet payments on a loan these can be sold off to repay the debt. Entrepreneurs usually believe that banks should take risks and see this practice as removing all risk. Lenders see things somewhat differently and, believing the security inadequate, often prove this by selling for a very low price if foreclosure is necessary.

Shareholders' funds The worth of a business that belongs to shareholders of a limited company. The assets less the liabilities. It is made up of the original investment by shareholders plus any revaluations of assets plus profits kept by the company after paying tax and dividends.

Start-up A new business is often referred to in this way. It refers to a business that has not traded before. It does not apply where a partnership is transformed into a limited company.

Synergy The idea, often mistaken, that by adding two businesses together the combination will do better than the total of the two individual businesses. Usually characterised as: $2 + 2 = 5$.

Turnover Income from sales of a product or service over a defined period.

Venture capital This describes all investment that is not covered by security (see 'Security' above). The investor shares the risk of the entrepreneur. If the business fails they lose their money. Entrepreneurs believe their businesses are certain of success and that the venture capitalist is seeking unreasonable rewards for little risk. The venture capitalist has many failed investments to try to forget and does not see things the same way.

Further reading from Kogan Page

Accounting for Non Accountants, 4th edition, Graham Mott
The Business Plan Workbook, 2nd edition, Colin Barrow, Paul
  Barrow and Robert Brown
Do Your Own Bookkeeping, Max Pullen
Financial Management for the Small Business, 2nd edition, Colin
  Barrow
How to Understand the Financial Press, John Andrew
Understand Your Accounts, 3rd edition, A St John Price
Understanding Company Accounts: The Daily Telegraph Guide,
  3rd edition, Bob Rothenberg and John Newman

Business Basics Series

Be Your Own Accountant
Budgeting for Business
Business Cash Books Made Easy
Cash Flow and How to Improve It
Controlling Costs
Costing Made Easy
Pricing for Profit
Taxes on Business